A Career in Contests

Morissa Schwartz

A Career in Contests

ISBN 9781463617219

All Rights Reserved

Copyright 2011 by Morissa Schwartz

Cover Art Copyright 2011 by Morissa Schwartz

Printed in United States of America

FIRST EDITION

To contact the author, email:

Morissa.Schwartz@yahoo.com

For book inquiries, email:

acareerincontesst@gmail.com

To my parents,

Mom, my best friend, the lady I will always strive to emulate, and the "wind beneath my wings"

Dad, who I am identical to in so many ways, the funniest person I know, and my superhero who "always has my back,"

~Thank you for introducing me to the art of contests~

Your New Career

In this rapidly changing world, there are more and more opportunities to make money through contests. There is a contest for virtually anything one can imagine and they are easily accessible, thanks largely to the internet. **Now** is the perfect opportunity for **you** to be the next big **WINNER.**

Contests are extremely profitable if done correctly. You do not need to get first place to benefit. As long as you are a finalist, you normally get a prize. A lot of money can be profited through contesting, if you utilize the correct skills. Contests are an extremely rewarding part-time or at home job that anyone can enjoy.

There are so many opportunities to make a profit in contests. Thousands of contests are online, for nearly anything you can imagine. Any talent you do or may possess can be turned into profit through contests. It is up to you to discover these talents and make a hefty profit from them.

Contests will require a lot of work, effort, and time. They are truly are a part time job. In some contests you will use your time to effectively use creativity and ingenuity to create something exceptional, while other contests will require you to spend a lot of that time attempting to gain votes.

Be sure to put your best foot forward when entering a contest. Always remember what is on the line. Often times, you will be entering for a prize worth a few thousand dollars. Think of how long it would take you to earn that in a regular job, when you begin to feel like you should not put all your time of effort into a contest. Sometimes a good contest entry may only take you a few hours and can earn you tons of cash.

To make a considerable profit in today's day and age, you will really have to focus on online contests. The contest world has changed a lot in the past few years. Even magazines and newspapers put their contests online. Online contests are much easier than mail-in ones. There are less forms, less mailing, and less hassle. In fact, many contest sites store your information, so you do not even need to fill out forms. Fill it out once and you're done. This saves you time and makes entering a lot easier. The more time and ease there is to filing out a form, the more time and effort you can put into your entry. This will likely increase your chances of winning.

When you win a contest, you can win a mountain of money, but more importantly, you become filled with pride. Every time you win a contest, it is like getting a promotion at work. You know that your hard work and talents paid off.

When entering contests and you start to become lackluster, just remember the three P's, which are the steps you must take in a contest:

- o PASSION: To get what you want in a contest, you must use all your efforts. You must enjoy yourself in the contest, or your entry will not be sincere.
- o PROFIT: As long as you get something in a contest, you profit. Even if you are just a runner up a million times, save up profits to earn that new car, cruise, or computer!

o   PRIDE: Be happy with your final
    product.   Be thrilled with your prize.
    Show it off to all your pals.

Why Should You Listen to Me?

Before introducing you to the world of all things contests, you first must know who I am. I have always been competitive. It is in my blood to enter contests. My mother was scholastically competitive and my father was a competitive athlete. I competed in my first pageant when I was only a year old and my first dance competition at age three. As I got older, it was only natural for me to make money through being competitive. I was never a real "professional contestant" until I turned ten, when I won my first grand prize: a giant sized "Coconut the Dog" stuffed animal from American Girl Doll Company. After that, I was hooked.

I started out as a sweeper (person who enters many sweepstakes), but the odds of winning were so much lower than that of contests, especially after online sweepstakes began to dominate. I began to use all my talents to enter contests, even ones I never knew I had. I enter every kind of contest, from essay to art, but my favorite type is videography.

Over the past seven years, I have entered thousands of contests. As I have become more experienced, I have won more. Now at the ripe old age of seventeen, I am a strong force in the contest world. Do not let my young age fool you into thinking that I am unknowledgeable in this subject, because that could not be farther from the truth. I have more knowledge and experience in contests than any adult I know, and I have even won dozens of **international** contests where my entries beat people five times my age.

Most people my age get jobs, but I do not need one, because I contest to make money. Contesting is like a part time job for me. I go to school weekdays and contest evenings and on the weekends. I win everything a person my age would normally buy. Everything I need for school, from school supplies to computers to scholarships, I win. But I am not just in it for the school supplies. I get fun stuff too, like iPods (I won nine of them), concert tickets, or gift cards. I even win an occasional prize for my parents.

Another aspect that I love about this new technologically savvy world is how I can always sell a prize online if I do not want it. I do not need nine iPods, so I keep one or two and sell the rest. When I win a prize, it is the equivalent to winning money, because I know I can just sell it for a huge profit on an online market place, if I do not want it.

I learned the best ways to win, the best kinds of contests to win, and what to do and not do when entering a contest. I win most of the contests I enter now, through this knowledge. I use my intelligible way to override luck, because sometimes you really can just make your own luck. In contests it's really not about luck, but knowing how to win.

I am a perfect example of how ANYONE can enter a contest. You can be young or old and still get the same joy out of contests and have the same chance of winning. Contests can even be enjoyed by the entire family. Let your daughter sing in your video. Have your aunt read that essay over for you. It's not just about the money but the experience.

Contest: Competition to Find the Best

Definition of **contest**:

Contest (noun): competition to find the best

This means that in a contest, you will be required to show off a particular skill to win a prize or money. There are many types of contests online. You can use old talents or discover new ones when entering contests. Explore the various contest types to discover which most interest you. Videography and essay writing are among the most popular types of contests, because a wide variety of people can enter these types.

You will need to explore all the types of contests out there. There are some very trivial contests that you can enter. Any talent or fun skill you have can be used in one of these. To enter a contest, you will most definitely need a computer with internet access. The best contests are really all online now.

The definition may say the contest is looking for the best, but there is nothing wrong with second or third best, especially if you get a prize. This is your new job. If your boss offered you a bonus that was the second largest in the company, would you be disappointed? No, you would graciously accept the gift and know that the person who got the larger bonus is at a slightly higher level then you. You would then work harder to achieve that level, so you could earn it too. Do the same with contests. Work harder to achieve first place after getting second, but be happy with the prize you earn for second.

Contests are NOT Sweepstakes

Contrary to the beliefs of many, there is actually a considerable difference between sweepstakes and contests. This book focuses on contests, because they have a much better success rate.

Sweepstakes are completely random. There are many different types of sweepstakes, but the most popular current type, involves filling out a form on a website and being entered into a raffle. This is not like entering a contest, because there is no assurance you will EVER win. Basically, entering a sweepstakes is like entering a free lottery.

Entering sweepstakes was not always that random, though. Only a few years ago, most sweepstakes were through "snail mail." You would put your name, birthday, address, and phone number on a small piece of paper or postcard and send it to the company that was holding the sweepstakes. Many would decorate the envelope to catch the eye of the people pulling the winning entrants, and those entries would win more often. Then, computers took over and success rates of frequent sweepers (people who often enter sweepstakes) began to drop. Since all the sweepstakes were online, they were strictly through chance.

Many more people enter sweepstakes than contests, because they are easier to enter. What they do not realize is that they are more difficult to win. You have more control over winning a contest. A contest takes skill, because it will require you to use a particular talent to win. Normally, these are fun talents, which are more like hobbies. If you like poetry, enter a poem in a contest and win a prize for it. It's like getting paid for just doing your hobby. Just like sweepstakes, in this new day and age, contests are normally done online. Unlike sweepstakes, this makes your chances of winning even greater.

Contests are much easier to win, because there are less people to worry about. First off, less people enter contests, simply because of the time it takes to devote to a contest. Second, many people's entries become disqualified. Do not worry, you will learn how NOT to get disqualified later, as this is half the battle in winning a contest. In actuality, contests actually take less time to win, because in a sweepstakes, it may take you weeks and weeks of mind-numbing filling out of entry forms, while a contest entry may take you a few hours.

Contests are a sport. It is not always just about the prize, but the pride of entering something that can give you recognition for your talents. There are so many different types of contests that anyone can find at least one type they are good at to win. Winning a contest is similar to the feeling of getting a promotion at work. You feel such overwhelming pride.

How Do I Get Skilled in Entering Contests?

To enter a contest is one thing, but to actually be a "professional contestant" is completely different. This book will introduce you to a wide variety of different types of contests, the best ways to win, and how to make money winning them. The best way to gain skill is by knowing what to look for in a contest. Know what your strengths and weaknesses are. Take every advantage you can. When you utilize all these skills, you will be a pro in no time. As with anything else, excelling at something takes time and practice, but will pay off in the end.

The more contests you enter, the closer you will get to becoming a "professional." Even if you do not win, every contest you enter gives you experience and knowledge. Learn from each contest you do not win. What prevented you from winning? If you come in as a finalist, but not a winner, figure out what you did well and what you could use improvement. Check out what the winner did and emulate them. When you do win, remember what you did right. Figure out the flaws of your opponents and if you should change anything next time.

Make Some Moolah

Remember, in a contest, you are competing for a prize that is worth money. Let's say you are entering a contest where the grand prize is a computer valued at $1,000. How long would it take you to earn $1,000 at a "regular job?" More than the few hours a contest takes! So, take your contests seriously, but have fun with them. The time you invest in a contest will earn you money.

When entering a contest, try your best, but do not be upset if you do not come in first place. There are many winners in contests, meaning your chances of getting a prize are greater. Every time you get a prize, you are making money.

In most online contests, it is not all about first place, because there are many consolation prizes. Normally there are first, second, and third prize, but sometimes small prizes are given to the first people who enter or other similar promotions. When you enter a contest, there are good odds of getting a prize, even if it is a small one, like a t-shirt or a small gift card, because a prize is money.

Prizes in a contest are normally not small. First prizes can be worth a few thousand dollars. Often second or third place will get a gift card for a few hundred dollars or an iPod; no small money there. Every contest is different, but no matter what the contest, there is always a chance to make money. Save up that money to get what you really want.

Sometimes prizes in contests can be a little off the wall. The contests will try to be creative so they will give something custom or unique, in which case you may want to keep it to remember the contest. For instance, I once entered a Christmas contest where all the runners up received a voice message from elves. It was cute, clever, and funny, but worth nothing. If you are doing contests just for the money and have no interest in remembering the time you spent to get there, you are better off entering the big name contests, because it is the smaller ones that will give the "memory" prizes.

Public Votes v. Judged v. Half Public Votes/Half Judged

There are three basic types of contest: public votes, judged, and half public votes/half judged. Depending on the kind of person you are is which type you should answer.

In a contest with public votes, you will need to campaign for yourself. Get your friends and family to get you as many votes as possible. Social networking is a great way to promote it. If you have a large family, many friends, and are a member of multiple social networking sites with many contacts, you have a good shot at winning a contest determined by public votes. There are other ways to get votes like public forums, blogs, etc. Get out there and you will be found.

In a judged contest, you will really have to depend on your talents. If you have created something that you are extremely proud of and sure can beat the rest, a judged contest is for you, because the judges will pick the best.

In a half public votes/half judged, there is a variety of ways that they can be run. In the first type, the entrants with the most public votes move onto the final round where the judges vote. In the second kind, the judges vote and after they narrow down the finalists, the public votes for the top winners. These types of contests are good for people with a lot of talent and contacts.

The Perfect Time

While contests have been around for many years, they have never been as accessible as they are now. Most contests can be done right from your computer. Long gone are the days where the **only** way to enter an art contest was through waking up early in the middle of July and showing off your prized painting at the local fair. Now you can scan that same painting onto your computer and upload it into an art contest website, where it will be judged for a prize. But you still have the **option** of entering your art in the fair. This balance of the "old world" and "tech world," gives you more opportunities to enter contests, meaning you have more opportunities to win prizes and make a profit.

Plus, online contests are gaining popularity and there are more for you to enter each day, meaning there will be an overwhelming amount of possibilities for you. One of the best ways for a brand to promote itself is through contests. I am sure you know at least five people who have entered an online contest. Ever get a little "vote for me" or "vote for my cousin" message on

Facebook? That was from that person entering a contest. Now that you are going to be a professional contestant, you should never delete those messages. Vote for your friend, or her cousin, or whoever is asking you to vote, because pretty soon, you will need their votes.

Plus, contests are popular, but they are gaining popularity. You should take advantage of the lack of competition while you can. It has been my experience that there can be anywhere from thirty to a thousand contestants in a contest, but as more people gain knowledge of contests, there will be a greater number of contestants. Take advantage of not everybody knowing about contests while you have the chance. It was a well kept secret for a while that is really blowing up, through social networks, and will continue to grow.

It is not necessarily a bad thing that so many people are now entering contests. The more people that enter a contest, the more prizes there normally are. As I said, it is not all about first place. As long as you get a prize, you have profited. Anything to increase your chance at winning a prize is a positive.

Ask the Moderator

In a contest, you are not alone. Any questions or concerns you may ever have can be handled by the contest moderator or "mod." Depending on how large the contest is that you are entering is how accessible the moderator is. In a large contest with many entries and large prizes, there will be multiple moderators and perhaps even a message board so you can see other people's questions and the moderator's response. In a smaller contest, you will have to search long and hard to find the moderator, but there will always be one. Often, you can find a "contact" link, where you can email the moderator any questions or concerns. The moderators can take anywhere from a day to a week to respond, so be prepared to wait. Also, if a moderator does take very long to respond, you can look up the company's phone number or main email, and ask someone how to get in touch with the contest moderator.

Most questions should be answered in the "rules and regulations" section of the contest, but if you have a question that is not, you may want to ask the moderator. Also, if you have trouble uploading an entry or accessing a part of the website that is crucial to your entry, the moderator will help.

The moderator is your new best friend in contests. He or she will always be there to help you and they may even moderate multiple contests that you enter. They may also be the ones to inform you that you have won. Moderators are very important in how well a contest runs.

Who is Hosting the Contests?

Normally, larger companies or brands hold the contests. It is simply a great, cheap way to advertise for them. It allows the consumers to gain interest in the product, while promoting their product for them. Therefore, contests are a win-win. The company gets "free" advertising, while you get a "free" prize.

Sometimes contests are held by private organizations. For example, the veterans organizations may hold a scholarship contest or an artists club may hold an art contest. The basic concept is still the same.

When you enter for a contest, aim your entry at the company. If you are entering a contest held by a women's clothing store, do not aim your entry at men. This will not go over well with the company, who wants to promote itself through this contest. If you send out the wrong message about their organization, they may even disqualify you.

Each contest is different because of the hosts. Just like people each contest has hosts with unique personalities. Here are a few you may run into:

The Easy-Going Small Time Contest

- **Traits:** These contests are "laid back"
  and do not take it as seriously as many
  other hosts. They may just be running the
  contest for promotion, but may not really
  know what to do or not really care. They
  normally have a smaller prize, less people
  entered, and are held by a less-well
  known company. They will not be so
  quick to expel someone from a contest.
  Also, they are a little more lenient with
  the rules. If you make a video and go a
  second over the time limit, you will not
  be disqualified, unlike many other types
  (I still do not recommend not following
  the rules, because you never know who
  might disqualify you).

- **Pros:** There are fewer entries so less
  people to deal with.

- **Cons:** Unfortunately, the moderators of
  these types will take a while to answer

your questions, if they do at all, and there are fewer winners.

- **How Can I Tell:** A tell-tale sign of one of these contests is if it is run by a company you never heard of or a smaller company.

- **Example:** I once entered a contest, where I made a music video for a little known band. There were only about twenty entries. It was supposed to be a judged contest by the band, not public votes. When the winners were to be announced they were not. I gave them a few days and sent an email to the contest moderator. Weeks went by without hearing from them, so I found the band on Facebook, and asked when the winners would be announced. I believe they had forgotten about the contest, and stopped checking the contest email and website, because they quickly apologized. Then, they announced that they would be giving prize packages to EVERYONE who entered the contest, and announced me as the first prize winner, where I got a prize valued at a thousand dollars. That is why, sometimes, the laid back contests do work out in the end.

The Strict Ones

- The strict ones get hundreds or even thousands of entries, many of them extremely talented. They are held by big name companies who are looking for an entry to make their company look great. That is why they must weed out anyone not up to their standards. There are so many entries they must process, that they have no time for anyone who does not follow the rules, even if it is slight. They are prompt in announcing winners and really stick to deadlines.

- **Pros:** You can be sure that a moderator will answer any of your questions, that the competition will be fair, and that there will be many prizes awarded. When you expect to see announcements, they will be there.

- **Cons:** You cannot get away with anything. If you are a millisecond over the time limit on a video, you are disqualified. If you are a character off the word limit on an essay, you are disqualified.

- **Counter-Pro:** As long as you follow the rules, you will do great. Much of your competition will get weeded out, by not following the rules, which helps you a lot.

- **How Can I Tell:** If it is a well known company, with a professional looking contest website and a lot of entries, it is a strict contest.

- **Example:** I once entered a contest for a well-known television network. I was immediately notified when my contest entry was received, when it was approved, and when the winners were announced. They were so prompt, that they said the winners would be announced on July seventh, they were announced the minute the clock struck twelve and it became July seventh.

The Scam Artists

- These are extremely rare to find, especially if you are finding your contest through a good contest website, catalog, or listing, but they are still out there.

- **How Do I know:** If they ever ask you for any personal information other than name, birthdate, address, phone number, or email, it is probably a scam. You should never have to give out checking or credit card information and you should not have to pay for anything. If the company is one you have never heard of or one that is close to a name that already exists, those are surefire ways to know that it is a scam. Also, if the prize seems to be too good to be true, it probably is.

- **Example:** If a company called Donkin' Dunuts, and they are offering $1,000 to the first three entrants and a million dollars to the winner, it's pretty safe to say it is a scam.

The Deadline Extenders

- The deadline extenders will normally be held by a company that is not so well known. They will look like any other, but there will be a clause in their **rules and regulations** section stating that they have the right to amend the contest deadline. They normally extend if they do not get enough entries or if they want to reach more people.

- **Pros:** When the contest gets extended, they often add more winners and prizes so

that the people who were already entered
do not cause chaos.

- **Cons:** They may keep extending the
  deadline for months, so if you were
  expecting that prize, you will have to wait
  a really long time. Plus, it's frustrating
  when you have to wait for the results for
  so long.

- **How Can I Tell:** Look for any clause in
  the rules that may give them the right to
  extend the deadline.

- **Example:** I once entered a contest for a
  charitable organization. There was
  supposed to be one winner and two
  runners up. They were supposed to
  announce the winners in September, but
  they only had twenty-four entries, so they
  extended it another month. Only two
  additional people entered, so they
  extended it another month. This charade
  continued until February, when they
  announced that there would be one

winner and four runners up, after all the
trouble. By that time, I was just happy to
be a runner up.

Now that you've gotten to know the hosts, perhaps you
should...

Get to Know Your Competition

It all depends on the contest, but you can often see your opponent's work, under a "gallery" tab online. In that case, you can figure out what you have to do to "top" them. Also, if the contest is through a site that allows social networking, like Facebook or YouTube, you can contact them and become "voting buddies" so you can vote for each other in other contests. It is like calling a truce. Most people just won't understand when you ask them to vote for you in a contest, but a fellow contestant will normally be excited to.

You can learn from your opponents in any kind of contest, especially video. When you see your opponents' work, maybe you will notice something about the contest that you would not have otherwise. Allow your biggest competition to be your greatest inspiration.

Normally when you enter the contest, it will not be your opponent's first contest and you may enter multiple contests against the same people. It is important to learn about your competition. Every contest will be different, but it is a fair statement to make that you will run into at least one of these types while entering your contest online:

- **The "pro"**

    The "pro" is one who has entered and won many contests. Normally, you will enter more than one contest with them, because they enter every contest they can find. The "pro" is the one with all the best supplies used to make their entry; they have the HD cam or the best paint brushes. The "pro" is hardest to beat. They wait until last minute to enter so no one can get any ideas from their entry, but use everyone else's ideas to use to their advantage. The "pro" will be the one who will make you say "wow" when you see their entry.

    o How to beat the "pro"

      Learn from the "pro." Be creative and put your best effort in. Maybe even reach out to the "pro" and ask them for votes, if they are not in the same contest. Aspire to become the "pro," a force to be feared in the contest world. The more you follow these tips and enter contests, the quicker you will become a "pro." As with anything else, becoming a professional will take time, skill, and dedication.

- **The Beginner**

The beginner is new to the contest world and may not have the best quality, but they have the most passion and take the contest most seriously. They are highly motivated and excited about this contest. You will be starting out as the beginner, and you will be so excited to start your contest career.

   o How to beat the beginner

   Do not get too overconfident and underestimate the beginner's abilities. Counting the beginner "out," is wrong, because they tend to have very creative and unique entries that just may catch the judges' eyes. Make sure to channel your passion in your work too. Use all your assets to make a great entry and try your best. Do not ever forget that excitement and joy of entering contests, so you can keep the passion in your entries. As you grow as a contestant, your spirit should always remain high.

- **The "Joke"**

In every contest, there is always one entry no one takes seriously. Maybe it is the video with a black screen and captions that say a brand message or the photo of a pile of out of focus rocks. These entries just do not belong in with the high caliber entries. The threat comes in when the contest is based solely on votes. Then, if this person has enough friends to vote for them, they may actually win. It's unfair, but these are some of the wildcard situations that get thrown into contests. You must be prepared for anything and never get discouraged.

o   How to beat the "joke"

Outshine them. If they're getting so
many votes with their effortless piece,
impress others with your entry that took a
lot of hard work. If it's decided by judges
only, you can pretty much count them
out.

*Also, make sure they followed all the
rules. Chances are, they did not, in which
case the moderator will catch them and
they will be disqualified.

- **The "Friendly" Spammer**

At first, the "friendly" spammer is the contestant
who keeps putting nice comments on your entry.
When you get the first one, you're flattered, but
when you click to the next entrant, you see the
same complimentary message, and then you see
it on every entry. At this point, you should be
thinking that they good potential at being a good
voting buddy, but they may also be trying to
show off to the judges or trying to get more

views on their entry. Then, they start sending you messages to check out their entry and to tell all your friends. They begin posting inks all over your entries to their entries. This is called spamming, and can actually get them disqualified, depending on how much they did it.

- o How to beat the friendly one

    You often have an option of deleting or disabling their comments, but normally they would be caught long before this would be necessary by the moderator. The spammers are normally disqualified, but even when they are not, I have never seen one win. They normally lack quality, which is why they try to gain attention.

- **The Cheater**

    Uh-oh, someone got a million votes in one day? Unless they're the president of the United States, it is not so likely. If it is obvious that another entrant is cheating, they will be most likely caught by the moderator of the contest. If the moderator does not catch them, there is nothing wrong with asking the moderator to "check into the unusual activity," by clicking the "contact" button located on the contest page. No, you won't look like a poor sport. Why enter a contest if it is not fair, right?

Heed my Warnings

Do not pay to play

If you ever have to pay to enter a contest or sweepstakes, it probably is not worth entering. There are so many free ones, that when a contest charges you to enter it is probably not all it is cracked up to be. Remember, you want to make a profit, not cost yourself money. Writing contests are normally the worst with charging fees. There are many free ones, so look for those before you shell out the dough. Trust your gut. If you think they are holding this contest just so you buy their product to make your entry, you are probably correct.

You must understand why the company or organization is holding the contest. Nine out of ten times, it is for promotion and advertisement of the company. Therefore, they do not need to charge you, because this is like free advertising. They are hoping to get your money from you buying their product, not from you paying money to advertise for them. Does the National Football League pay the soda companies to play commercials during the Super Bowl? No! The soda company pays. So, do not let them take advantage of you, because in this case YOU are the Super Bowl, in this scenario.

Read the Rules

No matter what, READ THE RULES and read them carefully. This point will be made throughout this book. In the "Rules and Regulations" section of a contest, the companies can add anything they want, and it is up to you to protect yourself.

About fifty percent of entries in contests get flushed out, simply for not following the rules. Therefore look for:

o   *Extensions*

The first thing you should look out for is contest extensions. Most contests have a right to "extend" a contest period. There will normally be some small print stating so. This means that if the deadline for entry has passed and there are not a "sufficient amount of entries received," the company can prolong the entry due date or in some cases, cancel the contest all together. That is why if you see entry deadline: August 5th and it is August 4th with only five entries, you can expect an extension, if the rules state that they can. The companies need to reap the benefits from this contest just as much as you. If they get a low amount of entries, they know their "advertising" did not reach a high amount of people and will try to get through to more and more people. It is in your best interest to enter contests without the extension rule, but sometimes you will find a good enough contest that does have an extension. For example, there was a video contest that was supposed to have only one prize, but after extending the deadline, they added an additional prize.

o *Are You Applicable?*

Contests usually have age restrictions and other rules that allow only certain individuals to enter. If you do not fit these guidelines, do not enter. Be sure to read for restrictions like "18 and older" or "only open to Canadian citizens."

o   *Do What They Say*

Some contests will have rules that state you must use their product or say a particular phrase. Do not forget to do that or you will be disqualified.   Be sure to title and format your entry the way the company wants.

*There will be specific examples of rules and guidelines on how to follow them in upcoming chapters.

Don't be Naïve

Many people think all contests and sweepstakes are "rigged." They don't think it is "real" people winning them, but people who work for the company posing to be a winner. In most cases they are completely wrong, but for every hundred or so legitimate contests or sweepstakes, there is a "fake" one.

Did you ever get on of those pesky boxes that pop up on your computer saying something like "You're the millionth viewer of this page. You win!"? That is a scam. And it is that type of scam that makes people weary of contesting. But you can be educated about the topic, so you can judge which contests to enter. You can normally tell by reading the rules and regulations, if the contest is a scam. If there is any talk about purchasing something, earning points, or paying money, it is most likely a scam. If it seems too good to be true, it is probably too good to be true.

You should use widely recognized contest listings that will screen out the scams or only enter contests for companies you have heard of. Reading the rules can also tell you a lot about whether a contest is real or fake, so be sure to check for clauses that sound fishy. The more you contest, the better you will be at sniffing out fakes.

Ask Away

If you ever have any questions, ask! There is always a contest moderator. Online, you will normally see a "contact" icon right on the contest page. I once entered a video contest with rules that read "no music." I thought that was odd, because part of creativity in a video contest often includes adding original music, but I did not question the moderator. My video was bland without any music and lost to a man who sang and played music about his children. I did not understand how the man could have won, since the rules stated no music.

I later found out, after others complaining about this same thing, that music was acceptable, **copyrighted** music was not. That is when I learned whenever you have a question in a contest, go right to the source and email the contest moderator.

Age Specific Contests

It is pretty rare to find a contest open to all age groups. The rules will often specify what ages are applicable for contests. Therefore, you must figure out where you belong and maybe recommend some of the contests that you are not applicable to other friends and family. The most common age ranges include school age, 12-18, 14 and up, 18 and up, and 21 and up.

Never pretend to be part of an age group that you are not. There is a good chance you will be disqualified. If anything, recommend the contest to a family member who fits that age and encourage them to enter. It is always fun to turn a contest into family bonding time.

Which Contest is Right for You?

There are contests for virtually anything you can imagine. Figure out your talents and enter contests in them. This will make contesting fun for you and give you a good chance for your talents to be seen. If you are in contests solely for the prizes, be safe and stick with what you know. But if you want a great experience and are okay with not always winning, enter a contest in something you have never tried before. You never know, maybe you will discover a new talent. I am the last person someone would expect to enter an online rap contest, but I entered one, because I wanted to try something new. While I did not get first prize, I still earned movie tickets and the pride of trying something new.

You probably already have the type of contest in mind that you would want to enter, but take this quiz to see if there are any others that may suit you well. Pick the BEST choice only for each question. Then, tally all you're A's, B's C's, and D's to see what most suits you.

1. How old are you?

    a. Below 18

    b. 18-35

    c. 36-50

    d. 50+

2. What would be your dream job, if you could not have one in contesting?

    a. A journalist

    b. A lawyer

    c. An engineer

    d. A teacher

3. How many people live in your home?

    a. Just me!!!

    b. 4-6 people (including me)

    c. Just 2-3 people (including me)

    d. Too many to count!

4. Which adjective best describes you?

    a. Intelligent

    b. Outgoing

      c. Creative

      d. Caring

5. What is your favorite color from this list?

      a. Blue

      b. Purple

      c. Indigo

      d. Green

6. What is your favorite animal from this list?

      a. Cat

      b. Monkey

      c. Dove

      d. Dog

7. If you got $100, what would you spend it on?

      a. A new iPod

      b. A karaoke machine

      c. A new computer

      d. Gifts for your family

8. Pick your favorite onomatopoeia from this list.

    a. Pop!

    b. Kazam!

    c. Zip!

    d. Moo!

9. Which holiday is your favorite from this list?

    a. Veteran's Day

    b. Halloween

    c. Earth Day

    d. Thanksgiving

10. Which virtue do you most possess?

    a. Patience

    b. Confidence

    c. Loyalty

    d. Compassion

If you picked mostly:

A's:

You would be great at **essay contests.** You are intelligent, patient, and enjoy the art of words. You enjoy peace and quiet, but love expressing yourself. Essay contests will require your deep concentration and unique opinions to impress the judges.

Depending on your age, you can win a variety of prizes. For younger people, these prizes usually include money for college or educational trips. For people passed school and college, you may get money and a chance to be published in a well known publication.

B's:

You should enter **video contests.** You love being creative and are quite outgoing. You enjoy the company of others and are very fun. Video contests require you to use your great personality to catch the attention of the judges, so make sure to let your outgoing personality shine. Depending on your personality type, you can add a lot of yourself into your videos. Can you juggle, sing, dance, or do any other cool talents? Add them into your video!

C's:

You should enter **art contests.** You see things differently than others. You are extremely creative and always thinking. Art contests will require your great eye for detail and ability to make a completely unique piece. There are so many types of art contests, and so many can be entered online. So, get out your camera and take a photo of that great painting, sculpture, drawing, or whatever else you create!

D's:

You should enter **recipe/cooking** contests. You care about others and love to bring joy to them. When you can create something for many people to enjoy, you are thrilled. In a recipe/cooking contest, you will create something for the enjoyment of many and add your own personality into your creation. Add your own touch to your delicious creations. The judges will eat you up!

Essay Contests

Essay contests are great for anyone, because everyone has their own voice that they can write with. The most popular essay contests are for high school and college students for scholarships, but no matter what age you are, there will be great opportunities for essay contests.

In an essay contest, you will be given a topic in which you pour your heart out on a specific topic. Essay contests receive more entries than a lot of other types of contests, but a large percentage of those become disqualified. Here are some tips for NOT being disqualified by preliminary judges:

- Keep spell-check ON
  - o Entries with mistakes like misspellings or noticeable grammar errors will immediately be disqualified by the preliminary judges
- Catch judge's attention, starting with the title.
  - o Make a title that stands out from the rest. Use a thesaurus, I necessary, to come up with the most unique, inviting, and intriguing title imaginable.

- READ THE RULES (see next pages for example)
    - Follow the deadlines stated in the rules.
        - Even if you are a day late, your entry cannot be accepted.
    - Write only about the topic that is stated in the rules.
        - Do not use an old essay about dogs if the contest is about cats.
    - Do not go over the word limit.
        - Even if you are over by one word, you may be disqualified, so check your word count (normally located under the tools section of your document).
- Have someone else read the essay over for you.
    - This will limit spelling or grammar errors you may not have caught and may add additional insight to your topic.
- Read the essay aloud.
    - Focus on whether or not the words flow and check for additional mistakes you may have missed while typing.

- If it's anonymous, keep it that way.
  - o Normally, you will only put your contact information on the registration page. Do not include it on your entry unless it specifies you should. That way the contest remains anonymous and fair.
- Use proper essay structure.
  - o The preliminary judges will also be judging you on whether or not you have a complete essay. This includes an opening, two to three supporting paragraphs, and a closing. If your rusty and do not remember this structure, pull out your old English book or check out one of the thousands of websites devoted to writing a good essay.

If you follow all these rules, you will have a good chance of getting through to the next round, where you will be mostly judged for your content. Therefore you must be creative. Depending on the contest you are entering, there could be thousands of people entering against you. Therefore, you really need to make your essay POP! Come up with a catchy title, be unique, and let your creativity shine. These judges will be looking at essay after essay about the same topic, so you must do something that will catch their eye. Take chances and write something that YOU would like to read. If you would not want to read it, no one else would. Write about what you know, so you can write a lot about the topic. Add anecdotes, if the rules allow.

If possible, check out your competition or previous winning entries. That will motivate you and set your standards. Draw inspirations and ideas from them, but do not write similarly to them, or the idea will no longer be original.

The most important part of an essay contest is following the rules. All your hard work and effort goes to waste if you break even one rule, so here's an example of a Rules and Regulations section, with extra italicized notes.

"The Debate" Essay Contest Rules and Guidelines"

Submissions Accepted January 5 - February 10, 2010

Rules for Mailed/Electronic Submissions

You will often see separate sets of rules in essay contests, one for mailed and one for online or "electronic" submissions. This is because many schools enter these contests, so it is easier to mail the entries together through regular mail. Individuals normally enter online for convenience, but you also have the option of mailing it in.

If mailing entry, submit three copies of an original work on the topic question. To electronic and mailed in entries, be sure to include an MLA format title page and MLA sources.

BAM! About 25% of entries just got disqualified right there. First, you must submit three copies. No, the contest company is not being greedy and wanting you to waste paper. They need a copy for each judge. Without the three copies, the judges cannot judge your entry, because they certainly do not have time to make copies of all the entries they receive. Next, include MLA formatted title page and sources. Don't know what MLA is? Look it up! There are tons of examples online. Last, be sure to include citations (sources) or you will be disqualified for plagiarism.

2. Submit one completed registration form signed by you. This may be printed from the contest website.

Remember, no registration form, no entry. How do you expect them to contact you if you're a winner? If you enter online, just type your name in the signature box upon registering, and that is your "virtual signature."

3. All submissions must include a word count, excluding the list of sources and the registration form signed by you.

Do not forget little details like this, or you will be disqualified. It's very easy to find the word count (you do not have to sit there reading every word), if you are using a program like Word, word count is two clicks away (tools, followed by "word count").

4. Entries must be typed, double-spaced, in 12-point Times New Roman or an equivalent font with a one-inch margin on all sides of the page. MLA format must be used.

You can have the most genius works ever written, but if you do not follow these directions, you will be disqualified. Be sure to get familiar with the program you are using, so you can format properly. The judges can tell if you types in 11-point Arial so do not test them. Just stick to the formatting rules.

5. Do not place your name on any of the pages of the essay. That information should only be on the registration form.

This is so that the contest remains fair. Everything in the essay is completely anonymous, so no one has an unfair advantage. This way, the judges do not have any favoritism towards any entrant.

6. Your essay will be disqualified if it does not meet the requirements or is postmarked after the submission date of February 10, 2010.

I warned you. There it is, right in the rules. YOU WILL BE DISQUALIFIED, if you do not follow the rules. So follow the rules and be prompt.

And there you have it. Follow those rules, and you have a good chance of being a finalist or winner, meaning you will win a prize.

Where DO I find these Essay Contests?

Depending on your age is where you will find the contests.

Students:

Essay contests for scholarships are your best bet.

- **Fastweb.com-** After you input information about yourself, like age or nationality, FastWeb will find scholarships that match your criteria. Most of them are scholarship contests. They list a variety of national essay contests, all judged by panels of esteemed judges.

- **Scholarships.com-** Similar to Fastweb, this website lists many essay contests for scholarships.

- **Cappex.com-** Similar to **Fastweb.com** and **Scholarships.com**, this website lists many essay contests for scholarships.

- **Locally-** Schools and local organizations, like the VFWs, Scouts, and Rotary Clubs, have many essay contests just waiting for you!

For Adults:

- **Writer's Digest Magazine and Writersdigest.com** are great outlets for writing contest that can earn you a lot of prizes and pride. It takes a lot of skill and practice to win one of these contests, but there are many tips here and links to other contests. Some of the contests they endorse charge you, but there are many free ones.

- **Writingcontests.wordpress.com** lists many writing and essay contests, mostly for adults. It is a good place to find contest listings.

- **With a quick Google Search of "essay contests," you are sure to find of plenty of contests that you can enter, which are updated daily.**

Video making

A popular favorite is video making, because every video can be completely different, depending on the company. Bob's Cookie Company may want a video with a catchy jingle in it, while Ralph's Horror House may want the scariest short video imaginable. The possibilities are endless.

To enter a video contest, you do not even need experience in video making, just passion and a camera, phone with built in camera, or a webcam. Some will tell you to invest in a good camera, but you should first try to win one. When I started out video contesting, I was a little fourteen year old with my dad's old camera that had a video recording function but was really meant for photography. While some contests do judge the videos on "clearness" or "video quality," the most important part of the video is creativity. Therefore, you can start out without a high end camera and work your way up to a more professional camera. When I first started entering, I would get high scores for creativity and low for technicality, putting me in a finalist, but never a winner position. As a finalist I would get smaller prizes, like cheaper iPods, small gift cards, or VIDEO CAMERAS. No, these video cameras will not be the thousand dollar type, but they are better than whatever you are using. Plus, you can always sell it on eBay and add in your own money to get a great video camera.

It is wise to enter contests for video recorders, when you are starting off, because those who are holding the contest, will recognize your potential. I won my new camera after I entered a contest that allowed you to enter through webcam, so that they were judging just on your ideas and not technicality. The contest was for Kodak, so all the prizes were cameras. It was the perfect contest for beginners that brought my contest entering to a new level.

You do not need to be a "videographer" to win a video contest. You actually do not need much experience at all, because most of the contests are for amateurs. The videos you make for most video contests will be like commercials for the company holding the contest, meaning you can make an original, fun video that has brand messaging. This way, the company gets "free" advertising.

Another good type of video making comes from showcasing your talents or hobbies. Do you like to sing? Then make a video and send it into a video contest for singing. If you play an instrument or are a comedian or have another talent, you can probably find a video contest for it. You can enter virtually any video you would put up on YouTube into a video contest; you just have to find the right fit.

Read the Rules and Regulations

The "rules and regulations" will normally be pretty long, some up to a dozen pages. While it may be tiring to read all these rules it is pretty important, because they will outline some things you must do that you would not normally know.

Here's an example of a video contest "rules and regulations." This will give you a better understanding than anything else of what a video contest is like, because it explores multiple scenarios you will run into when entering a video contest. This particular example is for a video contest that is half judged and half votes. It is a good type of contest to enter if you have a great video and a lot of friends, but that is not necessarily the only way to win. Read on to find out more. I have added notes to help you understand and to give you some helpful hints, in italicized letters.

RULES AND REGULATIONS
MS SODA COMPANY "BRIGHT DAYS" VIDEO CONTEST

While the title of the contest may not seem important, it is.   That is how you can let others know about the contest, if they need to vote, look out for it in the media, and tag it in the video if you are putting it on YouTube or another social media site, at the sponsor's discretion. Plus, it is a good way to get to know the theme.   If I saw this title, I would immediately think of including soda and a "sunny" theme in my video.   It would be a comedy or cheerful video, since "bright days" would remind me of that.   I may also think of making a beach or summer themed video.   Just from the title alone, you can get many ideas for your video.

NO PURCHASE NECESSARY. A PURCHASE WILL NOT INCREASE YOUR CHANCES OF WINNING A PRIZE. INTERNET ACCESS REQUIRED. VOID WHERE PROHIBITED.

Not only is this section legally required, it also is important to the entrant.   Some people think if they buy the product, it will increase their chances, but that would completely change the contest. Some contests will ask you to buy their product and feature it in the video. That would look something like this:

THERE IS NO ENTRY FEE FOR THIS CONTEST, BUT TO BE ELIGIBLE, YOU MUST PURCHASE A COPY OF <u>A CAREER IN CONTESTING</u> FOR \$9.99 FROM *MS BOOK SHOP* AND FEATURE IT IN YOUR VIDEO.

While this is fine, I normally enter the COMPLETELY FREE contests, because I can be more certain it is not a "scam," just to get me to purchase something. Companies normally hold contests to promote themselves, and that promotion alone gets them a lot of business from advertising. Be sure the contest is legitimate before you do buy something for the contest. I bought something for a contest only once. It was a song that needed to be purchased and featured in a music video. After reading the rules, I was certain that it was not part of a scam, because the rules protected MY rights, so I bought the song and entered.

OPEN TO LEGAL US RESIDENTS (EXCLUDING RESIDENTS OF PUERTO RICO AND US TERRITORIES) 18 YEARS OF AGE OR OLDER.

You must read this, so you know if you are eligible. I once worked for days on a video for a contest, to win a car, only to realize I was ineligible, because I lived in the US, and it was only open to residents in the UK. Also, as a minor entering the contests, I must be very careful. Contests are normally only open to certain age groups: children 6-18, people 14 and older, and people 18 and older. Sometimes there will be other age groups, but these are the pretty standard ages. Most contests though, are for people aged 18 and older. As a minor, you should never enter a contest open to people aged 18 and older, because they will send you an affidavit to sign, when you win, where you WILL have to prove you are over 18. If you lied, you will be disqualified and lose your prize. Same goes for adults: do not enter contests for kids. You may think you are a "ringer," but if you win, you will most likely be found out, disqualified, and may even face legal charges if you did get any prize.

1. **ELIGIBILITY**: **The MS Soda Company "Bright Days" Video Contest (the "Contest") is open to legal US residents of the 50 United States or the District of Columbia who are at least 18 years of age or older as of the first day of the Contest only. Void in US Territories and Puerto Rico and where prohibited by law. Employees, officers and directors of Sponsor, Sponsor's franchisees, and their respective affiliated companies, parents and subsidiaries and their immediate families and members of their households (whether related or not) are ineligible to participate in this Contest. Each Contest entrant is referred to herein as a "Participant." All Participants under the age of majority in his/her state of residence must have the prior permission from his/her parent/legal guardian to enter.**

The first section, eligibility, expands on the rules of who can enter. As previously stated, make sure you live in an area where you can enter. Also, you normally cannot enter a contest if you work for the company, because if you won, instead of the company getting "good press," which is what they are out for, they will be questioned and thought of unfavorably. Even if you are just an immediate family member, (spouse, parent, sibling, or offspring) *of a person who works for the company, you cannot enter either, for the same reason. Another thing to keep in mind is if the company you or your family works for is owned by the company who is holding the contest. This means if you work for MS Grocery or Sammy's Toy store (which is owned by the guy who owns MS Soda Company), you cannot enter MS Soda Company's Contest. Probably the most important part of this, for many, comes in the last sentence, which states that even if you are under 18, you can still enter the contest with permission from your parents. Then, you would either have to say "My parents gave me permission to enter this contest" at the beginning of the entry, or get a "virtual signature" from them and add it to the registration form. It is important to find that clause in contests, so you never miss out on a great opportunity if you are not the right age for it.*

2. HOW TO ENTER CONTEST: To enter the Contest, submit a brief video (maximum 2 minutes) to www.mssodacompany.com (the "Site) between 12:00 pm ET on October 16, 2011, and 11:59 pm ET on November, 31 2011 (the "Submission Period"), about your ideal sunny day and follow the links and instructions to complete all the required fields provided on the registration form ("Registration Form") and upload your video ("Submission"). The statement "MS Soda makes my sunny day" should be made at the beginning of the video. All Submissions must be received by 11:59 pm ET on November 31, 2011 (the "Submission Deadline"). Sponsor's computer is the official clock for the Contest. All Submissions must meet the requirements from these Official Rules. By registering on the Site and entering Contest, you further agree to abide by and be bound by the MS Soda Company privacy policy and

statement of rights. If you do not agree to the privacy policy and statement of rights and responsibilities, do not enter the contest.

This is another very important section. When they set a specific time limit, it MUST be followed. Even if your video is only one second over the maximum time, you will be disqualified. That is why I normally keep mine 5 seconds UNDER the time limit, just in case I decide to add a new title or quick clip, it will still be under. Do not worry too much about the time limit when you are filming, though. If the time limit were 2 minutes, I would probably film about 5 minutes worth of film and edit it down from there, so I could be sure that only the best footage was included, and it doesn't drag on.

Next, is the entry start and end date, which I cannot stress the importance of enough. If you enter even five minutes after the contest is closed, it will not be entered. Now, there is strategy involved when deciding when to enter the contest. Entering towards the end is normally best, because often other entries will be posted and you can check out your competition. However, if it is a contest that will be voted on by the general public, the earlier the better, so you can rack up more votes.

Another good way to make sure the contest is legitimate is by their privacy policy. When you enter a contest, you must enter a lot of personal information, name, address, phone number.   When you win a big prize, you sometimes even have to release your social security number. The privacy policy will ensure that your personal information will not be released.

3. VIDEO SUBMISSION REQUIREMENTS:

You should treat this as an outline to making your video. Everything you need to know to make your video will be in here.

A. Submissions must not exceed two (2) minutes in length

As previously stated, DO NOT go over the time limit, even by a second.

B. Submissions must be in the English language depict the Participant having a "sunny day."

This, once again shows that the company really wants this theme followed. Make EVERYTHING in your video relating to the THEME.

C. Participants agree to and understand that Submissions will be made available to the public, including but not limited to posting on the Internet. Whether or not Submissions are published on the Internet, Sponsor does not guarantee any confidentiality with respect to any Submission.

This gives the company permission to post your video on their website or even in a commercial. That can be exciting to see your video nationally featured.

D. Participants are responsible for securing necessary consents, waivers, talent and location releases, and licenses for any visual

and audio material contained in the Submissions.

Meaning if you have some sort of talent contract that prohibits you from appearances like this, do not enter. This way, the company can be legally covered and prevents "professionals" from entering.

More importantly, it brings us to our next lesson. NEVER USE ANY MATERIAL WHICH DOES NOT BELONG TO YOU. That may seem like "common sense," but it is not always so clear cut. Let's say you want to add some music to your video. You cannot just add any random song you have on your radio or iPod. You must either make your song or find a public domain song, which often comes with good video editing software. However, some contests do not allow any music in your video, so look out for a clause in this section that says "absolutely no music can be used in video."

E. Entrant must comply with restrictions. One entry per household. Sponsor is not

responsible for any expenses incurred in the production and delivery of the submissions.

This is included so that someone cannot enter multiple times. You cannot make five videos and enter them in your mother, father, and grandpa's name. That would be cheating and you could be disqualified. Remember, they can track your IP address, so if they get five entries from the same address, they will know.

Do not expect a company to pay you back for making a video for them. Remember it's a contest, meaning there is a chance that you will get nothing. You cannot expect the company to just pay you back if you lose or get a small prize.

CONTENT RESTRICTIONS:

The Submission must not contain material that is unlawful, offensive, threatening, hateful, violates any applicable local, state, national or international law...

I did not feel it necessary to include this entire section. Unless you are a lunatic, you are not going to depict some horribly offensive act of violence in your video, right? Good.

4. FINALIST SELECTION: All accepted Submissions will be evaluated by a qualified panel of judges designated by Sponsor based on the judging criteria ("Judging Criteria") described below.

- **Creativity – 30%**
- **Originality – 10%**
- **Related to "sunny day" theme – 50%**
- **Overall appeal – 10%**

This is so important. It is a great reminder as to what your video should depict. You know they want your video to be creative and original, so remember to do something you think few people will do. When you hear "sunny days," most people would set their videos at a beach. Make yours different. You can set it at the beach, but maybe have a zany character there. Whatever you choose to do, make your video creative.

Also, make sure you STICK TO THE THEME. Do not set your video in a dark lit cave, because, obviously it is not sunny there. This will count for 50%, so you can have the most creative video in the world, but if it does not pertain to the theme, you will lose. You must understand why theme is so important to the sponsor. This is like advertising for them. Without the theme, the advertisement could be for anything. Plus, some people use the same video for contest after contest. By contests having a theme, they can rest assured that this will be an original video.

The overall appeal part is important too, because if you have a creative video that fits the theme, but was made with horrible quality, this can weigh you down. Work with what you have to make the most appealing video. If you are filming with an old webcam, make sure it is the best quality possible and make sure the creativity makes up for those lost points.

Any ties shall be broken by an additional judge based on the judging criteria described above.

The Judges, whose decisions will be final, will select 10 finalists which will be announced on the Site beginning at 12:00pm ET on December 4, 2011.

Remember, just because the videos are due on a certain day, does not mean they will make an automatic decision. It takes time, sometimes up to a month, for all the judges to decide on a clear winner. So, don't pester the moderator until after this date has passed.

5. **VOTING AND CONTEST WINNER SELECTION: Beginning at 12:01 pm ET on December 16, 2011, Finalist Submissions will be posted on the Site and can be voted upon by registered Site Visitors ("Site Visitors") until 11:59**

PM ET on December 20, 2011 (the "Voting Period"). To become a registered Site Visitor you do not have to submit a video, however you must enter your first name, last name, and valid email address as indicated on-screen. There is a limit of one vote per registered Site Visitor during the Submission Period. The use of any automated, robotic, repetitive, programmed or similar registration or voting methods not approved by Sponsor is prohibited. Any questionable activity that increases votes for a Submission will result in disqualification of all such votes or similar action. Sponsor reserves the right, in its sole discretion, to disqualify any Participant or Site Visitor who is suspected of tampering with the Submission, voting or selection process.

Don't say you weren't warned. If you are one of the fortunate top ten, do not cheat your way to a winner's spot. Most likely, they will track your IP and you'll be disqualified. Instead, organize a plan. Send out messages to all your Facebook friends, tell everyone at work, or tell mom and you can be certain all her friends will know in no time. Plus, some video contest sites have sections where you can get people to vote for you, like Onlinevideocontests.com. Just post the link to the contest site, the deadline, and a personal message, and your fellow contesters will vote for you.

The six (6) Finalist Submissions receiving the highest number of votes as of 11:59 p.m. ET on December 20, 2011 ("Voting Deadline") will be selected as Grand Prize Winners (each a "Grand Prize Winner"). In the event of a tie, a judge designated by Sponsor shall evaluate the tied Submission(s) based on the judging criteria described in Section 4 above.

The Grand Prize Winners will be announced on the Site following confirmation by Sponsor whose decision will be final.

Make sure you tell the people who are voting for you the deadline. People have a tendency for waiting until the last minute, so you can make sure they vote by telling them the deadline, and reminding them to vote, through email, text, or phone call. There can never be enough badgering when a contest win is on the line.

6. **GRAND PRIZE**: **Each Grand Prize Winner will be awarded a $1,500 MS Soda Company Gift Card (ARV $1,500 USD each). Taxes are the responsibility of Grand Prize Winner. Grand Prize Winner will be required to sign an Affidavit of Eligibility /Liability and Publicity Release and to taking delivery of prize at a date, time, and location specified by Sponsor. All finalists will receive a gift basket from MS Soda Company (ARV $150 USD each). In addition, the first 100 entrants will receive a "MS Soda Company" T-shirt.**

Ah, so now you know what you are working so hard for. That prize is what you covet and you will do anything you can to win the grand prize, right? But after you win, the work is not over. The company will email you all sorts of fun paperwork that you must return, normally within the week. Then, they mail the prize to you. And remember, this is income, so remember to pay your taxes on it. You don't want to be the next Richard Hatch, do you?

If you did not win a grand prize but were a finalist, good for you! Your work is done! All you normally have to do is wait for your prize.

The total value of ALL prizes available to be won in the Contest is approximately $9,999 USD. Odds of winning a prize depends on the number of eligible entries received.

Remember when you enter to try to figure out your odds of winning. If it is a big national contest, where people of all ages can enter and it was widely advertised, your odds will be slimmer than a contest you read in a local paper, open to senior citizens only. I once entered a contest where there was only one other entrant. It was only open to people who lived in my town and advertised only on the local access channel. Contests like that are a sure-fire way to get a good prize, although they may not be as fun as one that has hundreds of entries.

7. **GENERAL**: **The Contest Entities reserve the right to terminate, cancel, suspend and/or modify the Contest without liability and without prior notice if any factor interferes with its operation as contemplated by these Official Rules, including but not limited to any fraud, virus or other technical problem which corrupts the administration, security, or proper operation of the Contest. CAUTION; ANY ATTEMPT BY PARTICIPANT TO DELIBERATELY DAMAGE ANY WEB SITE OR UNDERMINE THE LEGITIMATE OPERATION OF THIS CONTEST IS A VIOLATION OF CRIMINAL AND CIVIL LAW. SHOULD SUCH AN ATTEMPT BE MADE, SPONSOR RESERVES THE RIGHT TO SEEK DAMAGES FROM ANY SUCH INDIVIDUAL TO THE FULLEST EXTENT PERMITTED BY LAW. The use of automated or third party software or another web site not approved by Sponsor in order to register or enter this Contest is prohibited. Any questionable activity that increases votes for a Submission will result in disqualification or similar action.**

You see that first sentence there? Well, that gives the contest the right to basically do anything they want if the contest is not going as well as they hoped. For example, if they have this clause and there were only two entries, they can either extend the contest until they get more entries or "cancel the contest, indefinitely." I just love that one. Therefore, be careful if you see a contest with only a few entries and you think you are going to win, because if they have this clause, they will make sure they get more entries, and your chances will likely decrease.

Once again, the cheating thing is brought up. If you want to win the contest, win it honestly. There are many sites that say they will provide you with "automated" votes or views, but that is dishonesty at its finest and you can get in huge trouble for that.

No cash or other substitution may be made, except by Sponsor, who reserves the right, in its sole discretion, to substitute a prize with another prize of greater or equal value in the event that a prize is unavailable or cannot otherwise be awarded as described.

If you don't like your prize, either do not enter the contest or sell it online. Do not ask the sponsor for a different prize, even if it is smaller, because that is rude and puts a bad taste in their mouth. I have only once entered a contest where they did not have the prize. I won an iPod Shuffle, but at that time Apple was coming out with a new line, so the Sponsor wound up giving me an iPod nano that was worth double the price. Score!

8. Official Rules and Winners List: **For a copy of the Official Rules (which shall be available after October 15, 2011 or list of Grand Prize Winners, which shall be available after January 1, 2012, please send a separate, self-addressed stamped envelope) to: MS Soda Company c/o Sunny Days Contest, PO Box 1016, Happytown, NJ 55555**

Okay, if you want to skip over that, you have my permission. Why you would want a copy of the rules or winners when you can clearly access them on the computer is beyond me. Legalities, legalities!

Where Do I Find these Video Contests?

- **Onlinevideocontests.com** is the perfect place to find great video contests. They are even filed by age, prize, judging, style, and due date. This is the best place to find video contests. They have a great screening process and any worthwhile contest is on there.

- If you are looking for a huge video contest, with a lot of entrants, go to **Youtube.com/contests** and enter one of those big brand name contests that usually have a lot of big prizes.

Talent Based Video Contests

Basic same rules apply for talent based contests as the rules for the others. In a talent based contest, however, you will have to be more trained in a specific area and will edit less. Depending on your skill, these will probably take less time, but they will be more competitive, with more "professionals" entering. Many of these will not just be for prizes or money but for contracts or performances. Examples of popular talents showcased in these types of contests are singing, dancing, modeling or stand-up comedy. Be careful with these types of contests, because in many of these, you have to pay to enter. Look for the free ones; it's worth it. The ones where you have to pay are normally either scams or for people looking for a chance to get famous.

For a skill based competition, half vote half judged is normally how it goes. The judges will pick the top five or ten and the votes will decide the rest. That ensures that only those with talent will be finalists and the most "established" artist wins.

Art Contests

There are so many types of art contests. Like video contests, you will often need to design something for a specific company, not just your own art. Art contests are contests that you have to be extremely careful with, because a lot of these make you pay to enter or they take the rights to the art you worked so hard on. This does not mean all art contests are like this, as many are extremely rewarding.

Most online art contests allow you to take good quality photos or even scan your art into the computer. Therefore, you should invest or win a good camera or scanner, so you may have a better chance at winning.

You can find an art contest for anything you make: paintings, drawings, sculptures, and much more. Even jewelry making is found in contests.

When entering an art contest remember to:

- Follow the rules.
    - o If the rules state that the dimensions of a painting must be 8" x 11", do not

send in an 8.5" x 12" painting. Judges can easily spot those technical details.

- Only use the materials allowed.
    - o If you are only supposed to use acrylic paints, do not try to pass your water colors off as acrylic. Use the right materials to bring you right to the top.
- Present your art in a way that is appealing.
    - o You could be the next Da Vinci, but if you have your art in a broken frame or take a photo of your art with other objects in the shot, you are not going to win.
- Be creative.
    - o Make your own original art. Do not just recreate something you saw at the museum. Make your art stick out, like something you have never seen before and do not be afraid to take a chance.

Where can I find these art contests?

- **Deviantart.com** is a great place to find all kinds of art contests art contests. They have everything from drawing, to painting, to jewelry making contests and a lot more!

- **TeenInk.com** is a great place for teens to submit drawings and photography. Plus, they have a chance to have their work appear in a national magazine.

*Depending on your artistic specialty is where you will find where to enter your art contests. A quick Google search of "painting contest" or "drawing contest for adults," should allow you to find many contests for your abilities.

Recipe Contest

Anyone who loves to cook can enter a recipe contest. They are great fun and allow you to share your everyday meal with others, millions of miles away.

Recipe contests can be done through writing, photo essay, or video. In writing, you will simply send in a recipe and you are done. In a photo essay, you will send photos of yourself making the food. In a video, you can have your own little cooking show and record yourself making your prized recipe.

Here are a few tips:

- READ THE RULES
    - Normally, there will be only certain ingredients that can be utilized. ONLY USE THOSE ingredients.
    - Be creative while following all guidelines.
- Recipe contests are often held by a particular brand who want you to showcase their product, so give them what they want!

- o Use their product the most, get the most pictures or recording time with their product, and mention their product a lot.
- Make it appealing.
  - o Presentation means a lot. No one wants icky mush, so make it look as good as it tastes.
- Create a great recipe name.
  - o Make your recipe stick out with a great name. It should be catchy, descriptive, and short.
- Research a little.
  - o Read cooking magazines and books to find the most popular ingredients and to gain insight into what the judges may be looking for.
- Make it accessible.
  - o Use only ingredients you know will be found at local grocery stores, because people will likely be remaking your recipe. If they can't find the ingredients,

they can't recreate your recipe. And isn't
that the whole point of a recipe contest?

Contests, Contests, and More Contests

If you can think of it, it's probably a contest. Here is a list of a few:

o   Radio

o   Trivia

o   Karaoke

o   Poetry

o   Short Story

o   Novel Writing

o   Music Writing

o   Comedy

o   Timed events (contest where you have a certain amount of time to do something, like a 72 hour film contest or if you only had an hour to write an essay for a contest)

o   Instrument Playing

o   Acting

o   Professional contest (nursing contest, clowning contest)

o   Gaming

o   AND MORE!

You can probably find an online contest for anything you can think of. Everything from singing to book writing has a contest just waiting to be entered. Be careful and remember these general tips for ANY contest:

- Try to enter free contests.
  - o There are so many free contests; you should never have to pay. If there is a contest that you do have to pay for, make sure it is legitimate and one that you will earn more than you pay for.
- ALWAYS FOLLOW THE RULES.
  - ▪ But you already knew that.
- Be unique.
  - o You must catch the judge's attention. Distinguish YOUR entry!
- Research.
  - o Keep up to date and be accurate.
- Practice makes perfect!

- o The more you enter, the closer you will be to becoming a professional.
- Prizes are money.

I Won! Now What?

Depending on how large your prize is or where your entry may be featured, they may ask you to sign an affidavit form, waiver, etc. This is exciting, because it means you officially won. That is when reality strikes. Make sure you sign and return everything within the allotted time, normally three days to a week, or your prize may be forfeited and given to the runner-up. That is why you must check your email daily like a mad (wo)man to see if you have won.

When you win a contest, it will normally take 4-8 weeks to receive your prize. If it takes longer than expected, there is nothing wrong with contacting the contest moderator and asking when you should receive it.

Go Enter and Win

There you have it. You have become an expert in the field of contests. Now go make some money, gain some cool experiences, and discover through contests!

Remember MY rules:

- o Always read the **Rules and Regulations.**
- o Do not pay to enter.
- o Stand out from your opponents.
- o Get to know the host and entrants.
- o Do not give up.
- o Remember what you are entering for.
- o Never get lazy.
- o Practice.
- o Prizes = profit
- o Go above and beyond!

The ABC's of Contests:

Advertise your entry to get votes!

Be passionate about your entry.

Choose contest you know you'll excel at.

Discourage should not be in your vocabulary.

Each entry should be better than the last.

Find contests with the best prizes.

Go for it and try something new!

Have fun and it will show in your entry.

It's never too early or late to become a contestant.

Just try your best.

Keep a positive attitude. You WILL win.

Listings of contests are a great way to find them.

Mail-in entries are so ancient, enter online contests.

Now is the perfect time to enter a contest.

Only enter contest for your age group.

Passion, profit, and pride are the three Ps.

Quit…not in your vocabulary!

Rules and regulations are so important.

Stay in touch with fellow contestants so you can vote.

Take your time to make a quality entry.

Under the guidelines will be a "Contact" button.

Very rarely will there only be one winner.

Work hard on your entry.

Xhosa is a beautiful language, but enter in English.

You will be the next winner!

Zap! You are now ready to be a great contestant!

CONGRATULATIONS!

www.ingramcontent.com/pod-product-compliance
Lightning Source LLC
Chambersburg PA
CBHW070203290526
45789CB00002B/899